AF674442

Fix your Phonics

Workbook Grade 4

Om KIDZ
An imprint of Om Books International

SYLLABLE COUNT

Count the syllables in each word and write them on the blanks below.

crab ____________

algae ____________

coral ____________

dolphin ____________

herring ____________

mackerel ____________

oyster ____________

porpoise ____________

octopus ____________

pufferfish ____________

BLEND BUILDER

Use the blends in the bubbles to make new words on the fish below.

WORD WARP

Jinx the Jellyfish needs help with the words below. Help her by writing 'er', 'or' or 'ar' to complete them.

tig ________

farm ________

auth ________

tail ________

calend ________

pill ________

gramm ________

emper ________

LETTER TWIST

Jinx the Jellyfish needs help with these words too. Write 'our', 're' or 'ure' to complete them.

theat ________

met ________

hum ________

cent ________

enclos ________

nat ________

h ________

agricult ________

'EAR' SOUNDING WORDS

Olga the Octopus needs your help. Look at the pictures and fill in the blanks with the correct words.

ear hear pear
wear bear year

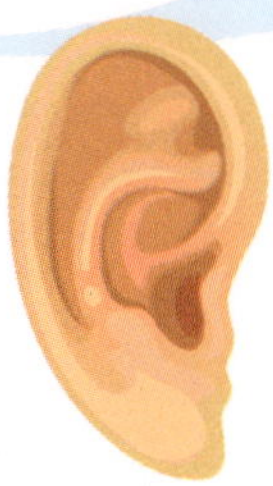

This is an ________.

We use our ears to ________.

The birthday girl will ________ a pink dress.

The ________ has a soft fur coat.

This is a leap ________.

My favourite fruit is a ______.

ADD 'A' FIX

Add prefixes to the words on the shells and suffixes to the words on the starfish. The clues below will help you.

____frost

____possible

____kind

____joy

____edible

high____

big____

run____

sad____

quick____

de im in
un en

er est ing
ness ly

THE LETTER 'L'

Suzie the Seahorse does not know where to use a double 'l' and where to use a single one. Help her by filling in the blanks with the correct number of 'l' below.

a ________ ow	ba ________ oon
gir ________	midd ________ e
be ________	hi ________
hote ________	scrabb ________ e

SIMPLE SENTENCES

Polly the Pufferfish is having a tough time writing words with 'ough', 'augh' and 'igh'. Help her to complete the sentences using the correct words from the river bed.

I have two lovely __________.

Have you __________ this jar of honey?

The lid on the box is __________.

__________, they say, is the best medicine.

Our teacher __________ us a lesson on marine animals.

The Dog Star is said to be the __________ star in the sky.

My baby brother is very __________.

Why does the moon come out at __________?

There is __________ petrol in the bus to take us for the picnic.

tight daughters night bought laughter taught enough brightest naughty

SOUND SORTER

Fill in the blanks with 'ove' sounding words. Choose words from the help shells.

When did the explorer ________ the new fish?

The dolphin is sticking its nose ________ water.

We bake a cake in an ________.

The white ________ is a symbol of peace.

The aquarium has a glass ________ around it.

Look at those two ________ birds.

CLOWN HUNT

Help the clownfish look for all the 'able' and 'ible' words in the grid below.

Q	A	F	Q	R	E	F	D	V	Q	V	A	Q
A	G	J	K	L	Q	S	E	L	S	G	A	R
S	V	Q	A	C	C	E	P	T	A	B	L	E
Q	Q	E	R	T	Y	Q	E	R	R	Y	U	D
G	S	R	E	A	S	O	N	A	B	L	E	I
Q	P	Q	U	S	U	Q	D	Q	O	S	O	B
C	O	M	F	O	R	T	A	B	L	E	Q	L
A	S	S	E	R	T	Q	B	Y	Q	N	P	E
S	S	Q	Q	E	S	W	L	I	O	S	O	Q
D	I	Q	W	Q	R	E	E	K	Q	I	Q	N
F	B	S	Q	E	Q	S	Y	Q	K	B	Q	S
G	L	K	K	N	V	I	S	I	B	L	E	C
Q	E	Q	Q	M	Q	D	G	S	A	E	V	X

Clues Across

When in comfort, you are...

When something can be accepted it is ....

When something is within reason, it is ......

When something can be seen, it is .....

Clues Down

When something can happen, it is ....

When something can be eaten it is ....

When you can depend on a person, the person is ....

If you have common sense, you are ....

FILLER FUN

Fill in the blanks with 'gh' or 'k'.

cau_____t	nei_____bour
_____nit	_____night
_____now	_____nife
throu_____	strai_____t
slei_____	li_____t

SILENT SAIL

Add some silent letters to complete the words below.

___nowledge

i___land

dou___t

wei___

si___n

s___ience

lis___en

___sychology

ta___k

bisc___it

'V' WORDS

Fill in the blanks with the correct 'v' sounding words from the seaweed below.

________ the wheat before you use it.

The colour ________ is a shade of purple.

Something that soothes or heals is called a ________.

The Sciatic is the longest ________ in the human body.

There's a sharp ________ along this road.

Let's ________ cheese and biscuits to our guests.

All animals ________ respect.

One must work hard to ________ one's goals.

mauve nerve achieve salve sieve serve curve deserve

DOUBLE LETTER WORDS

Snoopy the Starfish needs help to complete the sentences around him. Fill in the blanks using the words given below and help him complete the sentences.

________ is a state in the USA.

Jack is a ________ in our school office.

Work hard to be ________.

The ________ is meeting to make decisions about some matters.

The person to whom something is addressed is called an ________.

bookkeeper successful addressee Mississippi committee

'S' OR 'Z'?

'S' is pronounced as 'z' in some of the words below. Put the 'z' sounding words in Crissy Crab's basket.

news	was
has	birds
grass	days
busy	snow
safe	pass

SQUIRKY'S QUESTIONNAIRE

Help Squirky the Squid to write the correct words below.

What is the King's wife called? ____________

What is one-fourth of a whole? ____________

Where does a pet fish live? ____________

What do you call a line of people? ____________

When you ask about something,
what do you call it? ____________

What is another word for a fight?

____

'IE' OR 'EI'?

Jim is going snorkelling. He's gathering words that have either 'ie' or 'ei' in them. Fill in the blanks with the correct ones.

- v____w
- d____sel
- p____ce
- ch____f
- rec____pt
- s____ve
- rec____ve
- f____ld
- bel____ve
- c____ling

'K' SOUNDING WORDS

Read this news bulletin on the water board. Circle the words where 'ch' sounds like 'k'.

The school orchestra is going to perform on Friday at 2.00 p.m. The choir will sing Christmas carols. The anchor has asked all students to participate in the singing. Scholarships are also going to be announced that afternoon. The theme for the afternoon is orchids and other flowers. Flowers echo our feelings of oneness and beauty. We look for-ward to seeing students in the hall at 2.00 p.m. After all, unity is the chord that binds us all together.

GAME TIME

Use the following letters to make a word. Then use the last letter of the word to make the next word and so on. A word can have the same letter more than once.

z, e, r, a, b, f, i, h, s, d, g, o, e, c, t, s

zzzz

Joy the Jellyfish does not know how many 'z's to put in the blanks below. Fill in the blanks with the correct number of 'z's.

pu____le

nu____le

si____le

____oo

ja____

____ip

dri____le

pi____a

qui____

____ebra

FIND YOUR WAY!

Help this fish find its way to the bowl. Fill the blanks with words that have 'g' pronounced as 'j' and 'y' pronounced as 'i'.

I go to a ______ to exercise.

A ______ lives a nomadic life, travelling constantly.

To say sorry. ______

Not generous. ______

An Olympic Sport of flexibility. ______

A branch of science taught in schools. ______

biology **apologise** **gymnastics**

gym **stingy** **gypsy**

HOMOPHONES

Some words that are spelt differently can be pronounced similarly. Read the passage below and circle the words with the correct meaning.

We have too/to much to lose/loose if we do not protect our waters. Their/There is a treasure under the waters of our seas and oceans. There is a lot/allot of pollution and to/too many other issues to be addressed. When you see pictures of colourful corals and beautiful fish, they take your breath away. All our natural resources complement/compliment each other. It is therefore important that we don't make a desert/dessert of our natural beauty. Its/it's quite/quiet a big task that marine conservationists have taken up to ensure not only clean waters but also clean beaches and other surroundings. This matter is of/off great importance, so let's put our hands and heads together and save marine life.

WAVE MAKER

Fill up the boxes with words containing 'ui'. Two examples are given for you.

inquire	ruin

FLAG FRENZY

These children are making sand castles on the beach. Read the words on the castle and write their plurals on the flags.

MEANING MANIA

Match bubbles to their meanings on the right.

chateaux	The front of a building.
couture	A person employed to drive a car.
rapport	A large house or castle.
chauffeur	An artistic dance form.
facade	A wooden house, especially in Switzerland.
ballet	To do with fashion.
gateaux	A close and understanding relationship.
chalet	A rich cake.

HOMONYM QUEST

Dolly the Dolphin needs to find the correct homonyms. Fill in the blanks with the correct word from the bubbles.

We read from a _______.

We _______ tickets to watch a movie.

I got scared because I thought I saw a _______.

My cricket _______ is new.

I stood at the _______ of the river to see the fish.

My mother took me to the _______.

This is a _______ of baked beans.

_______ you please open this box for me?

_______ tastes great with bread and butter.

There's been a traffic _______ all evening.

book

bat

bank

can

jam

HOMOPHONE MANIA

Help Frida the Fish fill in the blanks with the correct homophones.

This ______ is sweet.

This is a ______ of shoes.

______ the clown fish there!

The ______ has a large variety of fish.

There are ______ many things to remember in phonics.

There are ______ chapters for our test.

Our teacher ______ us through the presentation.

Our teacher taught us about ______, a metal.

Please ______ after your performance.

The ______ on the tree broke because of the wind.

pair
pear
see
lead
sea
led
two
too
bow
bough

SEA SEARCH

Find and circle words with the letter combinations of 'ci', 'ce', 'cy' or 'ice' in the oyster grid below.

A	P	E	F	G	H	I	J	F
B	O	U	N	C	E	D	C	A
B	L	T	W	Y	A	R	B	C
C	I	U	X	Z	D	I	C	E
D	C	V	S	N	A	C	I	Q
E	Y	V	O	I	C	E	T	R
F	I	J	K	C	L	M	Y	N
G	H	N	I	E	C	E	P	O

WHIRLPOOL WHEEL

Sam the Sailor needs help to solve some riddles. Answer the riddles on his wheel to get words with 'wh' in them.

The largest sea animal it is!

____

Speak with a soft voice.

____

This makes your car move.

____

To go round and round like a circle.

____

The colour of peace.

____

A popular grain.

____

ANSWERS

Page 2

Page 4

Page 5

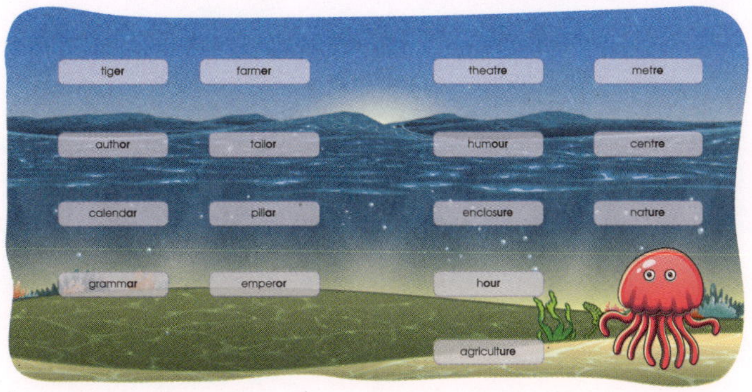

Page 6

This is an **ear**.

We use our ears to **hear**.

The birthday girl will **wear** a pink dress.

The **bear** has a soft fur coat.

This is a leap **year**.

My favourite fruit is a **pear**.

Page 7

Page 8

allow	balloon
girl	middle
bell	hill
hotel	scrabble

Page 9

I have two lovely **daughters**.

Have you **bought** this jar of honey?

The lid on the box is **tight**.

Laughter, they say, is the best medicine.

Our teacher **taught** us a lesson on marine animals.

The Dog Star is said to be the **brightest** star in the sky.

My baby brother is very **naughty**.

When does the moon come out at **night**?

There is **enough** petrol in the bus to take us for the picnic.

Page 10

When did the explorer **discover** the new fish?

The dolphin is sticking its nose **above** water.

We bake a cake in an **oven**.

The white **dove** is a symbol of peace.

The aquarium has a glass **cover** around it.

Look at those two **love** birds.

Page 11

Q	A	F	Q	R	E	F	D	V	Q	V	A	Q
A	G	J	K	L	Q	S	E	L	S	G	A	R
S	V	Q	A	C	C	E	P	T	A	B	L	E
Q	Q	E	R	T	Y	Q	E	R	R	Y	U	D
G	S	R	E	A	S	O	N	A	B	L	E	I
Q	P	Q	U	S	U	Q	D	Q	O	S	O	B
C	O	M	F	O	R	T	A	B	L	E	Q	L
A	S	S	E	R	T	Q	B	Y	Q	N	P	E
S	S	Q	Q	E	S	W	L	I	O	S	O	Q
D	I	Q	W	Q	R	E	E	K	Q	I	Q	N
F	B	S	Q	E	Q	S	Y	Q	K	B	Q	S
G	L	K	K	N	V	I	S	I	B	L	E	C
Q	E	Q	Q	M	Q	D	G	S	A	E	V	X

Page 12

Page 13

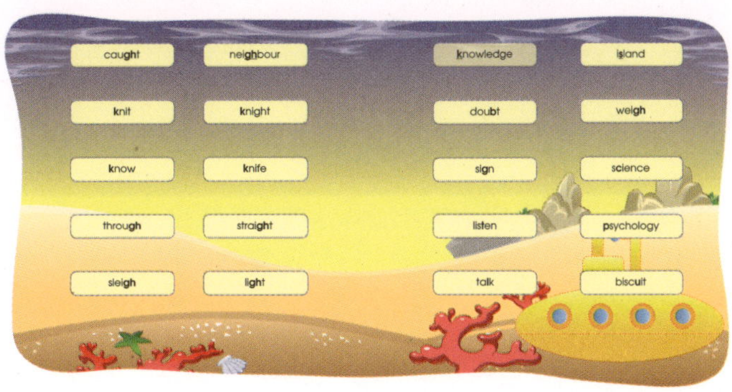

Page 14

Sieve the wheat before you use it.

The colour **mauve** is a shade of purple.

Something that soothes or heals is called a **salve**.

The Sciatic is the longest **nerve** in the human body.

There's a sharp **curve** along this road.

Let's **serve** cheese and biscuits to our guests.

All animals **deserve** respect.

One must work hard to **achieve** one's goals.

Page 15

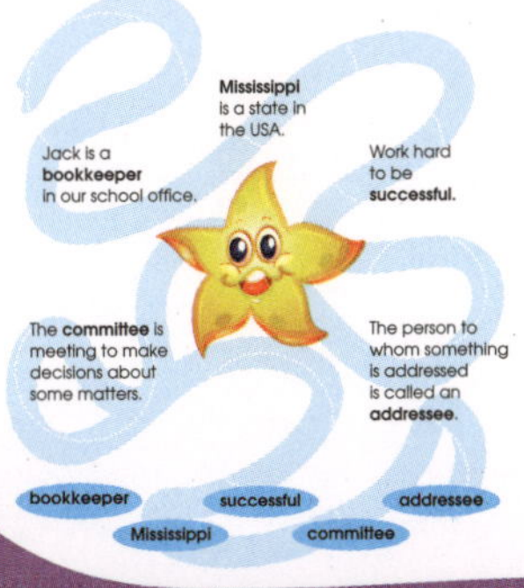

Page 16

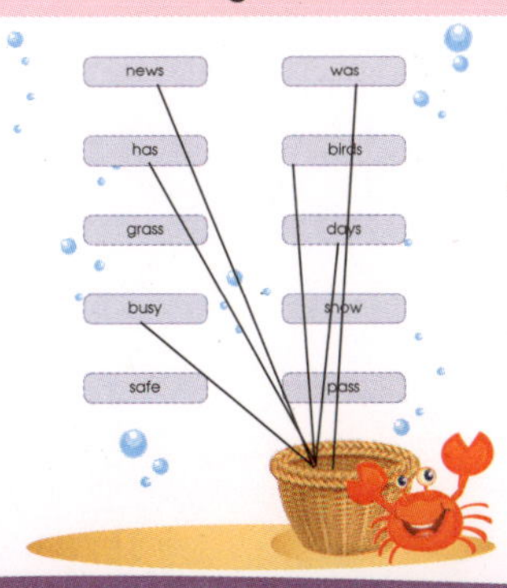

Page 17

What is the King's wife called? **Queen**

What is one-fourth of a whole? **Quarter**

Where does a pet fish live? **Aquarium**

What do you call a line of people? **Queue**

When you ask about something, what do you call it? **Question**

What is another word for a fight? **Quarrel**

Page 18

ANSWERS

Page 19

The school orchestra is going to perform on Friday at 2.00 p.m. The choir will sing Christmas carols. The anchor has asked all students to participate in the singing. Scholarships are also going to be announced that afternoon. The theme for the afternoon is orchids and other flowers. Flowers echo our feelings of oneness and beauty. We look forward to seeing students in the hall at 2.00 p.m. After all, unity is the chord that binds us all together.

Page 21

Page 22

Page 23

We have too/to much to lose/loose if we do not protect our waters. Their/There is a treasure under the waters of our seas and oceans. There is a lot/allot of pollution and to/too many other issues to be addressed. When you see pictures of colourful corals and beautiful fish, they take your breath away. All our natural resources complement/compliment each other. It is therefore important that we don't make a desert/dessert of our natural beauty. Its/it's quite/quiet a big task that marine conservationists have taken up to ensure not only clean waters but also clean beaches and other surroundings. This matter is of/off great importance, so let's put our hands and heads together and save marine life.

Page 25

Page 26

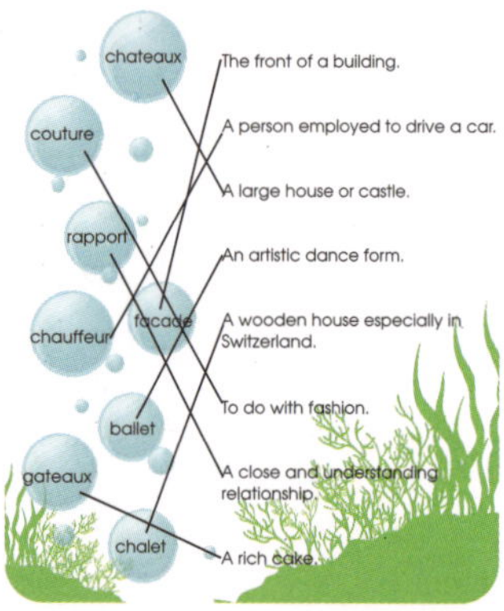

Page 27

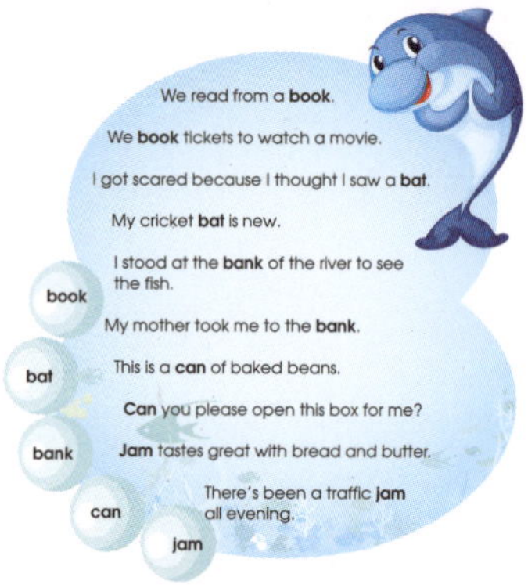

Page 28

This **pear** is sweet.

This is a **pair** of shoes.

See the clown fish there!

The **sea** has a large variety of fish.

There are **too** many things to remember in phonics.

There are **two** chapters for our test.

Our teacher **led** us through the presentation.

Our teacher taught us about **lead**, a metal.

Please **bow** after your performance.

The **bough** on the tree broke because of the wind.

Page 29

A	P	E	F	G	H	I	J	F
B	O	U	N	C	E	D	C	A
B	L	T	W	Y	A	R	B	C
C	I	U	X	Z	D	I	C	E
D	C	V	S	N	A	C	I	Q
E	Y	V	O	I	C	E	T	R
F	I	J	K	C	L	M	Y	N
G	H	N	I	E	C	E	P	O

Page 30

The largest sea animal it is!
Whale

Speak with a soft voice.
Whisper

This makes your car move.
Wheel

To go round and round like a circle.
Whirl

The colour of peace.
White

A popular grain.
Wheat